# Making Email Work For You...

*"We need to lead email rather than
email lead us..."*

nuggets

# Making Email Work For You...

*"We need to lead email rather than email lead us..."*

## Bev Wilkinson

nuggets

nuggets of learning

2018

First Printing: 2018

ISBN 978-0-244-64908-1

nuggets of learning Ltd
Bramley Manor
High Street
Bramley, Surrey GU5 0HS

www.nuggetsoflearning.co.uk

# Contents

Biography ...................................................... vii

Acknowledgements ........................................... ix

Why The Book Is Needed? .................................. 1

The Good, The Bad And The Ugly ........................ 7

Setting The Right Tone ..................................... 13

Effective Email Management ............................. 19

Ineffective Email Management .......................... 23

Getting Our Message Across ............................. 27

Next Steps – Booking A Workshop ..................... 29

# Biography

I help businesses to work and think differently by delivering unique training courses and coaching using the latest accelerated leaning techniques.

I design and deliver colourful, creative and memorable learning and development. You will know if you have been on a "nuggets" course. You will have practical outcomes but will have experienced a relaxed and fun way of learning.

Everyone is short of time so I deliver short development courses (90 minutes of learning) on a variety of topics.

I recommend 5 x 90 minutes of learning delivered each month with follow up coaching. I also deliver half day and full day workshops.

I also deliver executive coaching and motivational speaking.

Areas of Expertise:
Myers Briggs accreditation
Strength Deployment Inventory
CTi Coach

# Acknowledgements

**Matt Harris** who took all of our photographs, is a Surrey photographer who specialises in capturing natural, unobtrusive, honest and fun images. It's your story that he's here to tell, whether it's at your wedding, family gathering, event or the launch or rebrand of your business. (www.mjhpictures.com)

Without **Liz Sutherland** there would be no "Making Email Work For You." She has been brilliant at editing text and painstakingly positioning images. Liz has had a wide ranging career which includes International Banking in the City of London, running a catering company and IT recruitment. More recently she has been a Trustee of Kids Kidney Research and a Governor at Bramley Infant School.

# Why The Book Is Needed?

"*People don't read emails*" or is it "*People don't read emails properly.*"

How do you get your message across and how do you get noticed? We want to get attention for the right reasons, not because of a badly worded or structured email.

"*Anyone with an in-box knows what I'm talking about. A dozen emails to set up a meeting time. Documents attached and edited and re-edited until no one knows which version is current. Urgent messages drowning in forwards and cc's and spam.*"
Ryan Holmes  Internet Entrepreneur

When email entered the business world very few of us ever had training as to how to use it and very few companies have guidelines. The standard signature template is as far as it goes.

When information needs to be given quickly, there's no better way than by email. Less intrusive than a phone call, it empowers entrepreneurs to run their

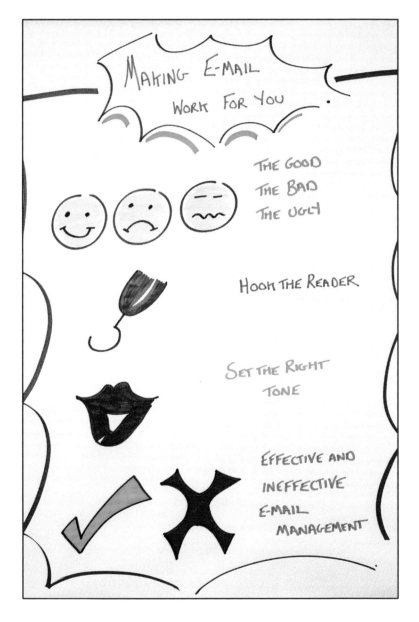

businesses from just about anywhere. Unfortunately with the benefit of speed come some problems that are not always predictable unless employees all use the tool in a consistent way that is true to the values of the organisation.

One quarter of a workers' day on average is spent answering and reading emails, according to research released in 2012 by the McKinsey Global Institute. Reading and responding to every message can become a drain on time and energy.

I was recently asked to design and deliver a workshop on how to make email work for you.

My client's brand and culture was very traditional and they felt their team did not reflect this in the way emails were worded and displayed.

You can relate this to the shift in Dress Code – more and more companies are opting for casual wear. Interpreting "*casual*" has proved tricky for some – too "*casual*" is bordering on positively careless – is this true of our emails?

On a practical level we need to lead email rather than it lead us. The last part of the workshop explored how to manage email effectively. The content of the workshop lent itself to becoming a "How To ?...Book".

# Making Email Work For You

The book is designed to be a guide to share with team members on how to be more effective with email. It is a practical resource for you to match your emails with your company culture.

In addition to the book we can design and deliver a nuggets workshop, tailored to your specific goals and issues.

The "Making email work for you" workshop has been delivered to several companies already. The changes that have happened as a result are, templates designed for standard emails, less emails internally and brand guidelines that include email. There have been personal changes for individuals as to how they interact with their in-box.

We recommend a 90 minute workshop with a maximum of 12 delegates. These short learning periods are highly effective for the brain to retain the information and most importantly less disruptive to your business.

The sessions are highly interactive with all the delegates engaged and involved. This means that not only do they "buy in" to the solution, but it is far more likely that the outcomes will be adhered to more rigorously and within a quicker time frame.

## The Good, The Bad And The Ugly...

We've seen the film and probably read the emails too – we know when things are bad and ugly but do we know what good looks like and how to achieve it?

> Good emails get their message across clearly so that everyone understands – see flip chart summary.

> Bad emails contain a few spoilers which dilute the message.

> Ugly emails are so bad the message is lost completely.

So much of communication is muddled, email seems an excuse to just release what is in your head with no thought for the audience.

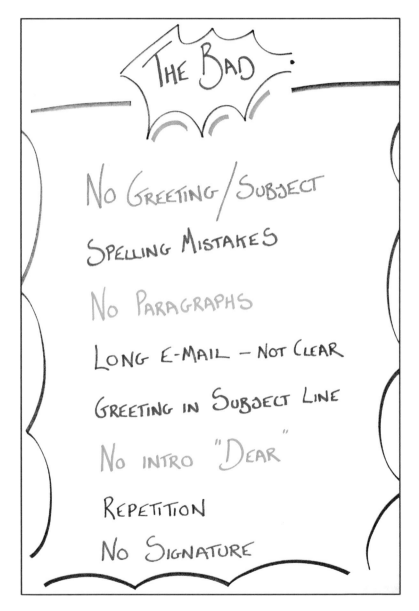

THE BAD

No Greeting / Subject

Spelling Mistakes

No Paragraphs

Long E-mail — Not Clear

Greeting in Subject Line

No intro "Dear"

Repetition

No Signature

Consider using the 7 "C's" model which can be applied to any form of communication and provide a very handy checklist to ensure clarity.

| Clear | Purpose |
|---|---|
| Concise | Keep it simple |
| Concrete | Say what you need to say |
| Correct | No spelling or grammar errors |
| Coherent | Logical |
| Complete | Next steps are clear |
| Courteous | The right tone and behaviour |

Courtesy of Mind Tools – www.mindtools.com

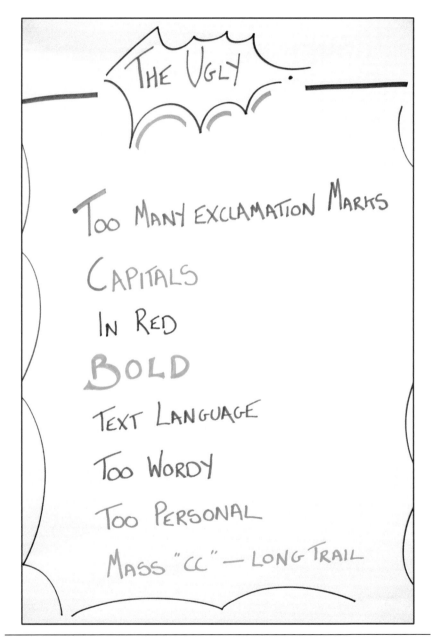

Knowing when to communicate and how to get a message across effectively is a skill in the digital age that we now live in. To cement relationships we need to steer away from the easy option.

The communication needs to be valid and memorable. Therefore we need to plan and prepare as we would with other forms of work.

# Making Email Work For You

# Setting The Right Tone

I am forever saying to my family, read the signals. We can gain a more meaningful connection if we look beyond.

Our emotional intelligence radar is about noticing changes in behaviour of others. When we observe people we have taken in the whole 100%. Their physicality is the largest proportion, it counts for 55%. We are looking for seepage in their body language – is there any leakage?

The leakage indicates a change in their state, how they're feeling about what you are saying or a trigger in their own head. The signals of change can be anything from a slight twitch, a massive change in their expression or a slight flick of the hair.

Tonality at 35% is another clue to watch out for – has their voice risen or gone softer? Does this give you the feeling of discomfort?

Words and language give us the final 10%, so when communicating by email we lose access to these clues and responses which makes it even more important to

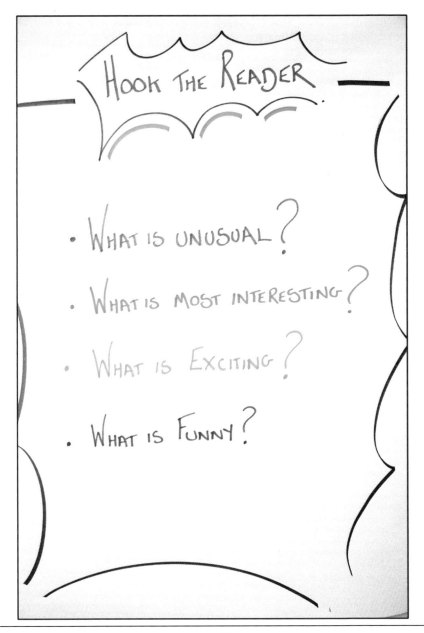

consider what you are writing, the tone you are using etc. to get noticed for all the right reasons.

**Capture the reader:**

Create a subject line that is a hook to the reader.

Headlines are very effective at hooking readers – they are intriguing, humorous, powerful and succinct. This is the same as a subject line in an email.

Take time to consider whether the subject of your email draws the reader in. Do not go for an easy option – be more creative. The brain always has to answer a question, so entice them to read on.

**Set the tone:**

Before you start writing...think

Preparing your tone in your mind is just as important as the words on the screen.

Companies need to decide is it appropriate to start an email with "*Hi*"? Is "*Kind Regards*" too formal?

Finding the voice of the organisation is about being in touch with your brand.

As an individual think about your own personal brand. Do you want to come across professionally?

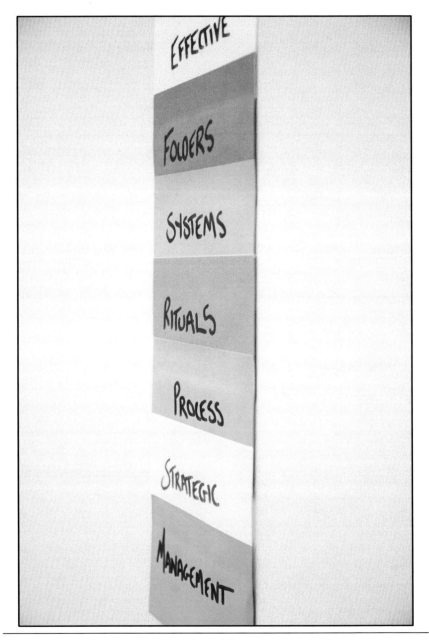

# Effective Email Management

*"We need to lead emails rather than emails lead us..."*

Bev Wilkinson

Being effective with email management is how you behave around emails rather than the simple processing.  We need to set ground rules and set up rituals and habits that fit with our lives. We can control it rather than it control us.

Dan Pink's book – "To Sell is Human", listed the number of emails he received in two weeks:

722 emails

To improve organisational effectiveness is not to focus on the number or volume.  The attention should be on clear guidelines as to how you manage your in-box.

There is no easy way and the whole idea of personal productivity means that it is personal to you.  Systems

EFFECTIVE E-MAIL MANAGEMENT

FOLDERS

FLAGS

CATEGORIES

BOOK AN APPOINTMENT WITH E-MAIL

SET CALENDAR REMINDERS

SAVE CONTACTS FOR QUICK REFERENCE

SET UP OUT OF OFFICE

MAKE A CALL – DON'T ALWAYS E-MAIL

need to be tweaked and adapted to work. Sharing ideas with team members can give you new ways of interacting with the screen.

If you look at an email 5 minutes before you go into a meeting you take that email into the meeting. Checking your email before you go to bed means that you will take that email to bed with you.

We can be effective by making choices that work for our lives, book an appointment with your emails as you would any other contact.

The book "Getting Things Done" by David Allen suggests setting up sub folders that sit at the top of your other folders. This can easily be achieved by putting a # in front of the title:

#Action
#Waiting for
#Read review

To be effective think about the rhythm of your day and decide when you want to manage your email. Relax that you don't have to know everything all the time. Being effective is the right processes for you.

# Ineffective Email Management

*"Email is not a technical problem. It's a people problem. And you can't fix people"*

— Merlin Mann

Imagine your email having no system, there would be no way of finding anything. It would be like opening your wardrobe with none of your clothes being on hangers just a pile of fabric to choose from.

In 2007 employees of Google gathered to hear Merlin Mann, a rising star in the personal productivity movement. He explained his system called "In-box Zero" - it was incredibly straightforward. People get into bad habits with email and check them constantly. Mann's concept was simple - everytime you visit your in-box you should process it to zero.

In-box Zero spawned countless blogs along with videos of people proudly sharing their empty in-boxes.

The irony was that In-box Zero did not bring calm, in fact it brought more anxiety. Some interpreted In-box Zero that every email needed a reply which meant more

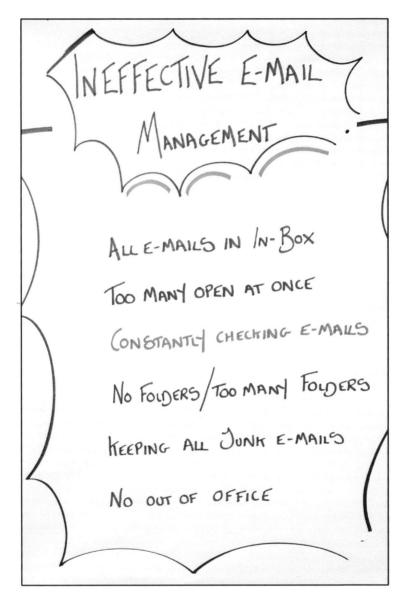

time in their in-box.  Others got obsessive on the whole empty concept so ended up checking more than before.  The super efficiency also ironically meant that by processing more emails you received more emails.

Two years after his Google talk Mann signed a contract for a book on In-box Zero.  The book missed its' publication date, then after a further two years Mann announced he was cancelling the project and was quoted

*"Email is not a technical problem.  It's a people problem.  And you can't fix people."*

Everything in life has to have a system set up, look at everything around you now, the files on your desk, your fridge, the cutlery draw and even the clothes you have on you.

Ineffective email management is no system and no control, you are being taken for a ride that you have not chosen.

# Getting Our Message Across

**Key *nuggets of learning* include:**

Hook the reader with a great subject

Start the message with the correct name and details

Set the right tone – be positive and professional

Ensure all your contact details are on your signature

Visually use a font that is appropriate for your company

Be effective with your email management – lead it

# Next Steps – Booking a Workshop

The book is designed to be a guide to share with team members on how to be more effective with email.

It is a practical resource for you to match your emails with your company culture.

In addition to the book we can design and deliver a nuggets workshop, tailored to your specific goals and issues.

The "Making email work for you" workshop has been delivered to several companies already.

Key **nuggets of learning** include:

> Reconsider sarcasm
>
> Apologise less
>
> Mind the BCC when forwarding emails
>
> Avoid "*I hope you are well*" – not specific or personal enough
>
> Action emails straightaway – no re-reading

Delegates have engaged with the interactive workshops, and as a result, outcomes are adhered to more rigorously and within a quicker time frame.

# Making Email Work For You